COTTAGE

GIFTS

THE COUNTRY CRAFT SERIES

COTTAGE
GIFTS

Mary Moody

CRESCENT BOOKS
NEW YORK • AVENEL, NEW JERSEY

Frontispiece: Fabric-covered boxes make beautiful gifts or can be used as decorative items for the home.

This 1993 edition published by Crescent Books,
distributed by Outlet Book Company, Inc., a Random House Company,
40 Engelhard Avenue, Avenel, New Jersey 07001

Random House
New York • Toronto • London • Sydney • Auckland

First published in 1992.
Reprinted in 1993.

Publishing Manager: Robin Burgess
Project Coordinator: Mary Moody
Editor: Dulcie Andrews
Illustrator: Kathie Baxter Smith
Designed & produced for the publisher by Phillip Mathews Publishers
Typeset in the U.K. by Seller's
Produced in Singapore by Imago

Title: Country Crafts Series: Cottage Gifts
ISBN:0 517 08797 9

CONTENTS

INTRODUCTION

Through this Country Craft series, it is our hope that you will find satisfaction and enjoyment in learning a new skill. In this case, that of cottage gifts.

The term 'cottage gifts' is used here to describe a wide range of practical and decorative household items made without sewing. It is an ideal hobby for those not adept at needlecraft, but who still relish the satisfaction of producing beautiful handmade gifts for friends or relatives.

Handmade cottage gifts can be seen displayed in hobby stores, or exhibited at craft exhibitions or fairs. Examples include a wide range of fabric-covered boxes and containers, covered mirrors and picture frames, lampshades, waste-baskets and covered address books and diaries.

However, the scope for imaginative and interesting variations on this theme is unlimited. Classes in gift-making are useful because they teach students the basic techniques and steps to assemble each article.

Most cottage gift projects are made from scratch using card, fabrics, batting and glue, plus a wide range of finishing accessories such as lace, ribbons, braid, tassels and cord. However, secondhand materials such as old shoeboxes, tissue boxes and recycled fabrics can also be used, keeping the cost of the craft to a minimum. Making boxes and containers using recycled materials has in fact become very popular, reflecting the trend towards avoiding waste and making use of every possible resource!

Unlike many other craft items, these handmade gifts do not have a particular history or tradition. They are really just a modern-day reflection of people's desire to make things by hand instead of buying mass-produced articles. Modern glues and spray adhesives have made the task of putting these projects together far more simple and also broadened the scope for the variety and scale of tasks that can be attempted.

One of the advantages of this craft is that it provides scope for individual creativity. Once the basic techniques are mastered it is possible to design your own projects, adapting them to your particular taste and requirements.

Not only are cottage gifts popular presents, they are also ideal fundraisers. Many are easy to make so that even beginners may quickly create attractive items for craft shows and markets. Groups can combine their resources to produce a variety of articles for such events.

Beautiful handmade items are a pleasure to own – boxes for storage, frames for favorite photographs, accessories such as wastebaskets for coordinating interior decor. Leftover fabrics that have been used for curtains, bed-coverings or upholstery can be made into coordinating accessories, giving a special finishing touch to bedrooms, living areas and kitchens.

Whatever the use, cottage gifts are easy and rewarding, even for the beginner.

GETTING STARTED

GETTING IDEAS FOR COTTAGE gift projects involves studying hobby books and magazines, and browsing around hobby stores for new concepts and inspiration. Once the basic techniques of the craft are understood, there is no limit to the range of ideas that can be developed.

Generally beginners stick to tried and trusted formats, following step-by-step instructions. However, once confidence has been gained, it is possible to design your own projects and experiment with a range of techniques and finishes.

A good starting point is a series of gift-making classes or a workshop. The cost of the class generally includes the basic materials needed for the project to be completed. It often works out less expensive to attend a one-day workshop than to buy the finished article in a craft store, so the lessons can pay for themselves from the first day. Workshops and classes offer invaluable advice on basic techniques, as well as providing helpful tips and shortcuts from the professionals.

Cottage gifts can be made on a kitchen table, requiring no special tools or equipment.

THE WORKSPACE

When working at home, it is a good idea to establish a separate working area where the projects can be left permanently setup. This prevents the tedious routine of packing up after every creative session.

Good light for working under is important, as well as adequate ventilation for when spray adhesive is being used. Glues can create a bit of mess, so the working surface should be well protected with layers of newspaper covered with an old sheet. Keep sharp and dangerous materials, such as scalpels, knives and adhesives, out of the reach of children.

Opposite: Trimmed with silk tassels and cotton lace, these hexagonal sewing boxes are covered in pastel floral cotton.

Simple but practical
gifts include a
stationery folder,
envelope holder
and covered box
for tissues.

CHOOSING A PROJECT

Always begin with an achievable project, such as the one featured in the back of this book. Plain, circular or square boxes, picture and mirror frames and covered books are all quite easy for beginners. Do not attempt difficult shapes, like hexagons, until you have gained confidence and experience.

CHOOSING FABRIC

Select fabrics that coordinate with the decor, or are in the taste of the person for whom the gift is to be made. Avoid very large patterns or designs for small items, as they will overpower the shape or become lost. Look for pure cottons or lightweight furnishing fabrics, and make sure you have the right measurements for the project, to avoid wastage.

Envisage how the completed project will look, to help with the selection of trims and accessories. Do not mix and match fabrics in any one project unless they are designed to go together. Too many colors and patterns will make the finished article look too busy.

GET ORGANIZED

Make a list of all the materials needed before starting work. Follow instructions carefully.

GLOSSARY

The following terminology is often seen in craft books and magazines when describing the techniques of gift making.

Card
The common term used to describe the cardboard used for making most cottage gift projects.

Craft glue
A clear, fast-drying, glue with various uses, including sticking boxes together.

Scoring
Not cutting, but incising part way through the card to create a fold.

Spray adhesive
Glue used for sticking fabric and batting to card.

Craft knife/Carpet knife
A knife that has a retractable razor-sharp blade used for cutting thick card.

Batting
A synthetic filling material used between the card and the fabric to give a project a padded form. The term 'bat' or 'batting' is also used to describe the action of inserting the batting, i.e. 'only bat the top and base of the box'.

A simple cotton-covered circular box
can be made from a kit available at most specialty hobby stores.

The basic cottage crafts kit includes a cutting mat, ruler, set square, graph book, scissors, knife, pencils, card, adhesive spray and craft glue.

TOOLS AND MATERIALS

MAKING HANDMADE GIFTS is a comparatively inexpensive hobby, even if all the tools and materials used are purchased new. However, it is possible to use secondhand and recycled materials that will reduce the financial outlay considerably.

Very few tools are required, so the initial expense of equipping yourself is minimal. It is probably worthwhile investing in a few craft books or magazines that outline technique and give project ideas, with photographs and step-by-step illustrations. For those lacking confidence it may also help to attend a few classes or workshops.

BASIC EQUIPMENT

Fabric Choose the right fabric for a particular project, to make an expression of individual creativity or taste. However, the better the quality of the fabric, the better the appearance of the finished article. Pure cotton fabrics are by far the best choice for making cottage gift projects. Those with a synthetic content, such as polyester and cotton blends, have a tendency to stretch or pull, spoiling the smooth, even finish of the work.

Cotton fabrics, from simple calico to beautiful Liberty prints, are all suited to the craft. Choose from plains, florals, plaids and checks – coordinate two or more fabrics into one project for a really interesting effect. Heavier fabrics, such as damask, brocade and tapestry prints used for upholstery, can also be used, but they are slightly heavier to handle. They are better suited to covering the outside of an item, with a lighter plain cotton used for the interior lining.

Fabrics can be found at hobby or fabric stores, and those who are keen can search through remnant baskets for interesting and unusual pieces to produce unique designs.

Trimmings The choice of trim gives scope for individual creativity. Laces, braids, tassels, silk cord, ribbons, dried or fabric flowers and brass corners are all possible accessories for the craft. Most of these trims can be found in hobby or fabric stores, or by hunting through odds and ends at fairs, markets or rummage sales. Look for unusual and interesting items to incorporate into a project, to give it individual appeal.

Card Both heavy and light craft card, available from craft suppliers and art stores, are needed for many projects. The thicker card is used for the main framework of the project, while a lighter card is often used for the lining. It is possible to use recycled card, such as cereal packages, for the lining. Secondhand boxes, such as shoe boxes, can also be used for the main framework of a project, although they are more difficult for beginners to assemble.

Pre-cut boxes Many hobby stores carry a range of card boxes that are already cut out, ready to cover and assemble. These certainly save time, but they are more costly than cutting out a box from sheet card.

Batting Many projects are batted with a synthetic craft batting which is the same material used for filling patchwork quilts.

The batting is available in bulk or by the yard at hobby and fabric stores. Medium to light batting is preferable.

Scissors   Two pairs of scissors will be needed – one for cutting card templates and one for cutting fabric. Do not confuse them, as cutting card will quickly make the scissors blunt, rendering them useless for accurately cutting the fabric.

Craft knife, scalpel   A craft knife is used for heavy duty cuts in materials such as heavy card; a scalpel is used for delicate, precision cutting of light materials. Both are required to make clean cuts; both should be used with care. Even sharp scissors will not accurately cut through thick card to leave a crisp, clean edge.

- Always cut in a direction away from the body. Always cut away from the hand that should be securing the material firmly to the work surface.
- Never, ever, hold an item in your hand to cut with a knife; if the blade should slip then you **will** cut yourself.
- Keep all the tools sharp
- Keep all tools from inquisitive fingers.

Rubber mat   Use a rubber mat to protect the table when cutting through the thick card with a sharp knife. The cutting boards marked with squares are also useful for checking that edges are straight and that right angles are exactly square.

Ruler, set square   Accuracy is vital for the success of cutting out the shapes to be covered. A ruler marked with both metric and imperial measurements will make converting patterns and designs from various sources much easier, and a set square will insure that the corners are straight.

Pencil, fabric marker A sharp pencil is used for drawing the outline of the design onto card, and also for marking the fabric outline. A fabric marker may be preferred for this task.

Craft glue, spray adhesive   Lookout for environmentally-friendly adhesive spray glue with hydrocarbon propellant.

When handling glues always take precautions. Avoid contact with your skin, and never breathe in the vapors. As it is highly flammable, the adhesive spray should never be used near an open flame and should be stored in a cool place.

Craft glue is a fast-drying, clear adhesive, suitable for various applications. In general the spray adhesive is for applying the fabric and batting to the card, and the craft glue is for sticking the entire project together.

Pegs, rubber bands   Plastic clothes pegs are sometimes used to hold fabric and card together when tracing the design; or as clamps until glue to items has set.

A rubber band may be useful to hold a circular piece in shape while the glue is drying.

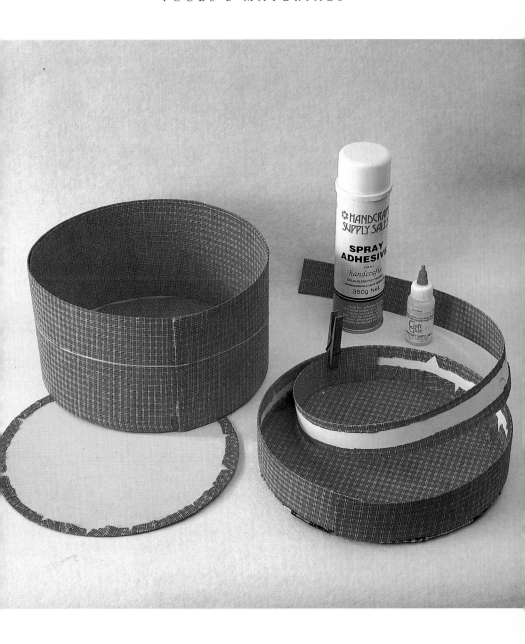

During assembly, pegs and rubber bands are used to hold pieces together while the glue adheres.

TECHNIQUES OF THE CRAFT

ACCURACY IS VITAL to the success of this particular craft. The careful measuring and cutting of the card and fabric will determine the success of each project. As with patchwork, inaccurate cutting will result in edges that do not meet, and corners that do not fit together exactly.

Most cottage gift projects are covered with fabric as they are assembled. The order in which the pieces are glued together must be worked out carefully in a logical sequence.

If a secondhand cardboard box is being covered it will need to be partially cut apart so that fabric can be glued around each edge. This is the only way to achieve a neat, professional finish.

Like most crafts, practise will bring better results. Start with small, simple projects, and practise the basic techniques before going on to more ambitious challenges.

CHOOSING A PROJECT
Ideas for individual projects can be derived from books or magazines, or by looking closely at finished works and seeing how they have been made.

The size of the item can be enlarged or reduced as required, and finishing touches can be varied according to taste. Once the

basic cutting and gluing techniques are understood and the order of assembly is worked out, there is scope for designing and making up your own projects. The ideas covered in the following chapter will give a clear idea of assembling most projects.

DRAFTING A DESIGN
If designing your own project first draw up a paper pattern to scale, on graph paper if desired, to get a clear picture of how the pieces will fit together. Use a ruler, set square and sharp pencil, measuring with great care and accuracy.

If a pattern has been supplied in a book, it should already have a scale drawing from which to draft the design. If you imagine that you will be making more than one example of a particular design, cut out a template that can be used over and over again to cut a fresh batch of card. It helps to label each template with a name and number by which it can be identified. This is particularly important when making a lined box, for example, as the surfaces are often a similar shape and size, and can be easily mixed up.

The lining surfaces are generally just slightly smaller, and are covered after the exterior surfaces. Some surfaces are to be batted, and

Opposite: A small crochet doily has been used to trim the front of this padded address book.

An unusual fan-shaped
box in pale blue cotton,
topped with a floral fabric
and trimmed with braid
and a fabric rose.

*A pretty gift presentation stationery folder,
trimmed with lace and ribbon
and a padded heart.*

these should be labelled carefully – it even helps to write 'bat' on those pieces, to avoid confusion. As each card surface is cut out it should be labelled too, as a way of identifying each piece.

CUTTING THE CARD

The card for the main framework is quite thick and heavy, and will need to be cut with a sharp craft knife or scalpel.

Some patterns call for the card to be 'scored', so that it can be bent into shape when it is covered. This is done by running the knife along the measured line, only partially cutting through the thickness of the card. A rubber mat is a helpful accessory, because it helps to hold the card in place while cutting, and protects the surface of the table.

When cutting, follow the drawn lines exactly and make corners and edgings neat and sharp. Some experts recommend not cutting the card right through on the first stroke of the knife. Instead, run the knife along the cutting line, as for scoring, leaving a groove. The track of the first cut will act as a guide during the second stroke, when more pressure is applied; it should cut through the card neatly and accurately.

Keep in mind that these cutting knives and scalpels are extremely sharp, and should be handled with care. Store them away from the working surface when they are not actually being used.

CUTTING THE FABRIC

The fabric should be also cut with care, using clean and sharp fabric scissors. For most projects a 1/2 inch edging allowance is required for the fabric to fold over the edge of the card when it is glued.

Place the template or cut card shape on the reverse side of the fabric and use a fabric marker to draw around the shape accurately. When using dark fabric, a white marking pencil will be necessary, so that the outline can be seen clearly.

After outlining the shapes required, cut the fabric, making allowance for the turnover.

The fabric edge allowance must be snipped so that it will turn back neatly. This should be done before it is glued, using the drawn outline as a guide.

Do not snip right up to the line, but leave enough for the actual turnover. This edge-snipping is particularly important for fabric that is following a curved outline.

CUTTING THE BATTING

When making boxes, generally the top and the base of the inside are batted for additional shape and softness.

To cut the batting, first trace the shape from the card or template using a felt-tipped pen to mark the outline (the synthetic texture of the batting does not absorb pencil lines). The batting can then be cut out, using clean and sharp fabric scissors.

After gluing it is a good idea to trim back any overhanging batting that may have stretched slightly, to create a neater finish.

USING THE SPRAY ADHESIVE

One of the less pleasant aspects of this craft is handling spray adhesive, which emits fumes and can make a mess if not used properly. The spray adhesive is used for sticking the fabric and the batting to the card.

Make sure that the table is well covered and protected before beginning to spray, and spread a sheet of newspaper on top of the protective cover.

It is a good idea to use a fresh sheet of news-paper every time you spray, as some glue always manages to reach the paper and can stick to the next item being sprayed.

Shake the can well prior to spraying, and hold it about 10 inches from the surface to be sprayed.

Use smooth, uniform movements to insure the glue has coated the surface evenly, right up to the edges. Spray both surfaces to be adhered, i.e. both the back of the fabric and the card or batting.

Work swiftly and cleanly, keeping in mind that this type of adhesive dries quite quickly. However, if the fabric is not on straight, or has a bubble or wrinkle, it can be easily peeled back and repositioned without too much trouble if done immediately. Try to keep the surfaces as smooth as possible – remembering that if a section has been sprayed heavily it may show through the fabric.

Some manufacturers of spray adhesive recommend inverting the can after each session and pressing the activator, to clear the nozzle.

USING THE CRAFT GLUE

This clear craft glue is actually used to stick the various components of the project together, i.e. the sides of the box, the lid of the box. Like the spray adhesive it is also quite toxic and flammable, although it is slightly more easy to manage. Most brands have a nozzle top for ease of application.

Use the glue sparingly, although insure that there is enough to stick the pieces together firmly. It is important to stick right up to the edges without actually allowing any glue to be visible, and this takes a little practise. Use a matchstick to wipe away any glue that may squeeze out of the sides when the sections are pressed together.

Keep in mind that this glue is very fast-drying and there is not much time for fiddling or repositioning sections if they have not

been placed together evenly.

Work quickly and neatly.

FINISHING OFF

The project will need to be set aside to dry thoroughly, which takes about 12 hours.

Any final trims can be added after the drying period.

SUMMARY

Follow this sequence when making cottage gift projects.

1   Choose a project.
2   Draw a plan of the project on graph paper, labeling all sections and dimensions.
3   Cut out card shapes using a sharp knife and rubber mat.
4   Label all shapes to correspond with the drawn plan.
5   Cut out the fabric with a 1 cm 1/2 inch allowance on all sides.
6   Snip the edges of the fabric where it is to be turned over the card edges.
7   Cut out the batting, using the card shape as a template.
8   Use spray adhesive to stick batting and fabric to the card. Work quickly and neatly to achieve smooth results.
9   Use craft glue to stick the various shapes together in a logical sequence.
10   Leave the project to dry.

A charming padded circular box in maroon and pink floral cotton, trimmed around the lid top with silk braid.

STARTING WORK

THERE ARE MANY IDEAS to choose from in this rewarding craft. By setting out some of the more popular projects it is easy to see the various stages of assembly, so that the basic techniques can be adapted to whatever project you choose.

LINED BASKETS

Wicker baskets look very pretty when lined with a cotton fabric. Using fabric has both a decorative and a practical purpose, whether for storing knitting yarns or fabrics for craft projects, also, small items can not fall out. A basket of any shape can be lined.

The basic steps are:

1. Measure the depth and circumference of the basket. The fabric will need to be 4 inches wider than the depth, and twice the circumference.
2. Draw an accurate outline of the basket base, then cut this shape from thick craft card. Make sure it fits neatly before covering it.
3. Cut a piece of batting in the shape of the card base.
4. Cut a piece of fabric in the shape of the card, with a 1/2 inch allowance all around the edge.
5. Snip the allowance so that the fabric will turn back neatly when glued.
6. Spray adhesive onto both the batting and the card surfaces and stick them together.
7. Use spray adhesive on the batting and fabric. Stick them together, making sure the overlap is turned back neatly.
8. Hand stitch the fabric into a circle.
9. Fold the top of the fabric over to make a frill, and use a running stitch to gather it so that it fits the basket size neatly.
10. Spray the back of the fabric along the stitched line, and also spray the inside of the basket where it is to be fixed.
11. Press the fabric to the basket, arranging the gathered folds neatly.
12. Spray the underneath of the padded base and also the base of the basket.
13. Press the padded base into position, making sure that the side lining is tucked underneath carefully.
14. Leave the project to dry.
15. For a professional finish, a length of braid, ribbon or lace can be glued on the inside, along the line where the running stitch gathers the fabric.

Opposite: A wicker basket lined with cotton paisley fabric is ideal for storing sewing items.

Basic covering technique

To cover a basic shape like this hat box, first measure the fabric with 1/2 inch turn over allowance.

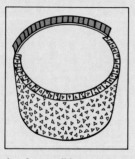

A circular shape will have a smooth finish if the fabric is snipped so that it does not buckle when the edges are glued over.

Use spray adhesive on the outside of the box, then use craft glue on the folded edges.

COVERING A BOX

Boxes of all shapes and sizes can be padded and covered with fabric to make beautiful gifts or decorative items for the home.

For boxes made from sheet card the basic steps are:

1. Draw the design on graph paper, labeling all sections and marking dimensions (this step is not necessary if the pattern is drawn in a book or magazine).

2. Draw up the exterior outline on thick craft card, taking care to be accurate.

3. Draw up the lining outline on a lighter thinner card.

4. Cut out both the light and heavy card shapes, using a sharp craft knife or scalpel.

5. Trace the shape of each section onto the fabric using a fabric marker or white fabric pencil.

6. Cut out the fabric using sharp scissors, and include a 1/2 inch allowance for turn over.

7. Snip the fabric turn over.

8. Use spray adhesive on the batting and fabric to attach them to the card. Cover the exterior of the box first, then add the lining panels.

9. Use craft glue to stick the box sides together.

10. Add finishing touches (ribbon, lace, dried flowers).

11. Leave to dry.

A heart-shaped box in crisp black cotton with a floral padded lid and base.
Note the appliqué flowers around the edge.

A circular box with an unusual lid trim
in plaid cotton – the patchwork design
is called, 'Dresden Plate'.

Finishing techniques and trims for basic boxes
can be quite intricate, like this rose appliqué
edged with black lace.

Covering a book

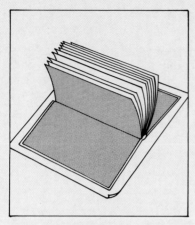

To cover a book, first cut the fabric with a 1/2 inch allowance around the edge.

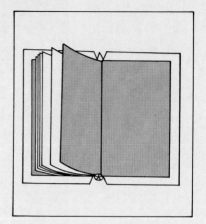

Use sharp scissors to make a V-cut at either end of the spine. Tuck the V-shape under.

COVERING A BOOK

Address books, diaries and notebooks can be padded and covered with fabric to great effect.

The basic method is:

1. Trace the outline of the book onto the back of the chosen fabric.
2. Cut the fabric to fit neatly on either side of the book spine.
3. Trace the outline of the book onto a piece of craft batting.
4. Use spray adhesive to stick the batting to the book, then to the fabric covering.
5. Turn edges over neatly on the inside.
6. Measure the dimensions of the inside cover.
7. Cut two liners from heavy paper.
8. Use spray adhesive to glue these to the inside, front and back to secure the fabric turn over.

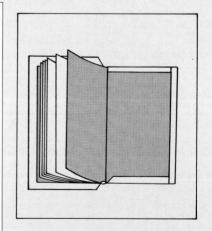

Use spray adhesive applied to the wrong side of the fabric to cover the outside of the book. Then use craft glue to turn over the edges neatly.

Covering a lampshade

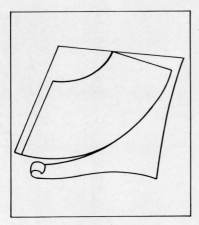

*Cut a pattern from paper,
using the existing seam of the shade as
a starting point.*

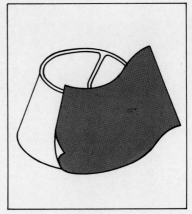

*Use spray adhesive to apply the fabric
to the shade. If renovating an old
shade, remove all dust before gluing.*

COVERING A LAMPSHADE

Use fabric to renovate an old lampshade to match other soft furnishings such as drapes or chair covers, or to cover a new frame.

The basic steps are:

1. Make a paper pattern of the lampshade by tracing down the existing seam and measuring around the circumference of the top and bottom.

2. Use the pattern to cut out the lampshade shape on the back of the fabric, leaving a 1/2 inch allowance on the sides for a small overlap.

3. Use spray adhesive on the back of the fabric to make it adhere to the shade. (If renovating an old shade make sure it is clean and dust-free before sticking down the fabric.)

4. A trim of some sort will be needed to

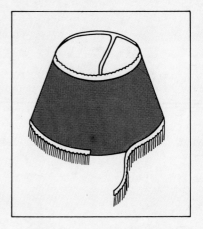

*Trim the shade with braid or fringing,
held in place with craft glue.*

cover the top and bottom where the fabric ends. Consider ribbon, braid, silk cord or fringing.

5. Leave to dry.

COVERING A WASTEBASKET

The same basic steps used to cover a lampshade can be used to cover a wastebasket.

COVERING A PICTURE FRAME

Photographs of all sizes can be framed using fabric and batting.

The basic steps are:

1. Cut out two rectangular or square shapes using thick craft card.
2. Cut out the same shape using a lighter, thinner card.
3. Cut a hole – oval or circular – in the center of one of the thick sheets of card, and also a hole to match in the lighter sheet. It is important that this hole is perfectly centered, or the frame will appear lopsided.
4. Cut out the fabric to cover the front and back of the frame.
5. Cut out a piece of batting to fit the front of the frame.
6. Both the batting and the fabric will also need a hole cut – the batting should have a hole the same size as the card, however the fabric hole needs to be 1/2 inch smaller all around.
7. Snip the fabric where it is to be turned into the hole.
8. Use spray adhesive to adhere batting and then fabric to the front of the frame.

Opposite: Diaries and notebooks look elegant covered in paisley, plaid or plain cotton.

Covering a wastebasket

Measure and cut the fabric to fit the shape of the basket.

Use spray adhesive to apply the fabric to the outside of the basket.

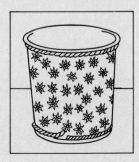

Trim with braid or cord, using craft glue.

9. Line the inside of the front of the frame with the light card.
10. Cover the back of the frame with the fabric.
11. Position the photograph and use craft glue to press the front and back of the frame together.
12. If necessary, cover a small piece of thick card and glue onto the back of the frame to make it stand up.
13. Leave to dry.

COVERING A MIRROR TILE

Making a frame for a mirror is similar to making a photograph frame, but instead of using card covered with fabric for the backing, a mirror tile is used.

The basic steps are:
1. Cut out two card squares the same size as the mirror tile, using thick craft card.
2. Cut a circle in the center of one sheet of card.
3. Cut out the fabric to cover the front and back of the circular frame.
4. Cut out the batting to fit the front of the frame.
5. The batting will have a hole the same size as the card hole. However, the fabric hole needs to be 1/2 inch smaller all around to allow for the turn over.
6. Snip the fabric so it can turn over the edge of the hole neatly.
7. Use the spray adhesive to fasten the batting and fabric to the front of the frame.
8. Glue the mirror tile onto the second card square.

Opposite: Craft glue is used to trim a lidded basket with lace, shells and painted fir cones.

Covering a picture frame

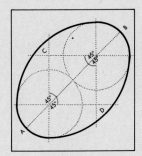

Use this simple method to draft a perfect oval shape to cut from the center of the rectangular card frame.

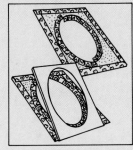

Use batting on the outside of the frame between the card and fabric. Use a second piece of card to back the frame.

The back of the frame is not padded. A simple card support can be covered in fabric and glued if required.

Covering a mirror tile

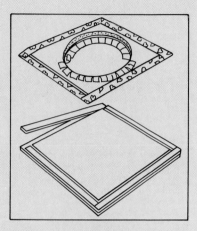
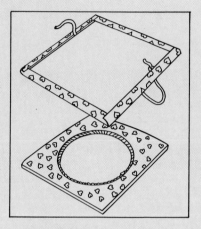

Make a neat circle in a square of card, then use batting and fabric to cover it. Glue the mirror tile onto the second cardboard square, edging it with 1 inch strips of card for stability.

Cover the back of the mirror with fabric, then glue the two sections together using craft glue. Trim around the mirror circle with braid and cord, and use the matching cord to hang the mirror.

9. Cut 1 inch strips of card and glue them around the edges to give greater strength to the card.

10. Cut a fabric square to cover the back of the mirror. There will be a 1/2 inch turn over allowance.

11. Glue the fabric to the back of the mirror tile and turn over the edges. Snip to neaten and fit.

12. Glue the mirror tile with fabric back to the circular frame using craft glue.

13. Trim around the mirror circle with braid and cord. Use cord to hang the mirror.

Covering a tissue box

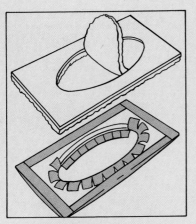

Use the card oval on the top of
a box of tissues as a pattern.
Cut a rectangular card shape and
cover using batting on the top.

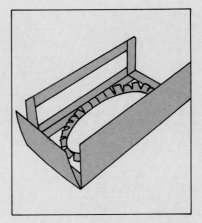

Cover four rectangular sides, then
glue them together with craft glue.

COVERING A TISSUE BOX

Dress up a box of tissues with a fabric and batting cover that fits neatly over the top. This is an excellent project for fund-raising events and fairs.

The basic steps are:

1. Trace the outline shape of the top and sides of a tissue box. Trace the shape through which the tissues will emerge.

2. Draw this shape onto thick craft card and then cut out.

3. Trace the outline of the top onto a piece of craft batting, including the central oval shape. Cut out the batting.

4. Use the card to trace the outline shape onto the back of the fabric. Cut out fabric with a 1/2 inch turn over allowance. Snip the allowance around the hole to insure it turns back neatly.

5. Using spray adhesive, cover the top of the box first, inserting the batting and taking care when turning in the edges around the oval.

6. Cover four sides of the box with fabric.

7. Glue the four sides to the top neatly and carefully.

8. Leave to dry.

FINISHING TECHNIQUES

IT IS POSSIBLE TO ADD finishing touches to assembled projects to tidy up the edges or simply for decorative purposes.

TRIMS

Braid, ribbon, silk cord and lace are all used as trims for various cottage gift projects. In some cases the trimmings are added during the assembly process; however in other instances they are glued in place when the project is completed.

Do not overdo the use of trims, as this can make the finished article look fussy. If the fabric itself is busy with a colorful pattern, then no trim may be required.

Plain fabrics, calico or cottage prints, will often, look pretty with some braid or ribbon trim, and the total effect on the finished item will not be overpowering.

FLOWERS

Dried or fabric flowers can be used to decorate boxes or baskets. Craft glue should be used to hold them in place, and they need to be positioned one at a time. Do not make arrangements of flowers too large or too bulky, overpowering the size and shape of the article being decorated. It is important to keep a sense of proportion.

GOLD EDGES

These are often used to trim the lids of boxes, giving them a neat and professional finish. They are generally added after the box has been glued together, as a finishing touch.

Opposite: Boxes can be covered to match existing decor using scraps of fabric left over from bedcovers, drapes or cushions.

Notebooks and albums can be trimmed with gold corners to give a professional finish.

BEGINNER'S PROJECT

Designed by Janice Powell

COUNTRY-STYLE BOX

This charming lidded box has been designed to fit neatly around a box of cotton wool squares, although it could be easily used to store any personal treasures.

The edges of the lid have been trimmed with neat gold corners, and the lid is opened with a gold cord and bell.

MATERIALS

16 inches fabric
5   inches very fine gold cord and small bell or tassel
1   Sheet of thick craft card
    Small amount of craft batting
4   Gold corners (optional)
    Craft knife
    Scissors, ruler
    Craft glue
    Spray adhesive

A simple fabric-covered box with gold trimmed edges and a gold bell tassel for easy opening.

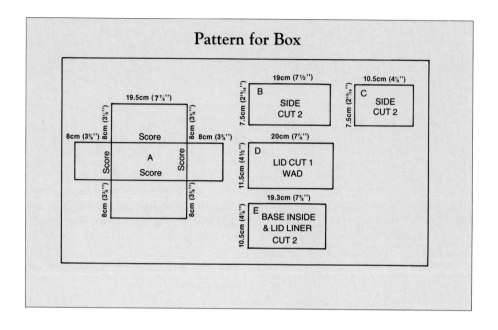

Pattern for Box

METHOD

1. Cut A, B, C, D & E to the measurements shown, from thick craft card. Score with a craft knife as indicated on A.

2. Cut the fabric for all pieces with a 1/2 inch allowance on all sides.

3. Using spray adhesive, cover all pieces of card with fabric, batting D only (this will form the top of the lid).
   When covering A, remember that the scored side of the card is glued to the wrong side of the fabric to create the base and sides of the box. Glue the corners first.

4. Glue two C inside liners into the box, and one B side.

5. Glue the four edges of the box together.

6. Cut a piece of fabric 6 x 2 inches to use as the hinge of the box.
   Spray adhesive on the wrong side of the fabric and fold in half. Glue half of this piece to the uncovered inside of the long side of the box, then glue in the remaining B inside liner.

7. Glue bell and cord to the center front of the long inner side of the outside batted D lid. Glue the back of the inside lid D flush with box to remaining hinge fabric.

8. Glue in the lid liner, then glue on four gold corners if required.

A floral padded address book, trimmed with cream cotton lace.

INDEX